PORTRAIT OF AN ARTIST

FRIDA KAHLO

ILLUSTRATED BY **SANDRA DIECKMANN**
WRITTEN BY **LUCY BROWNRIDGE**

WIDE EYED EDITIONS

Magdalena Carmen Frida Kahlo y Calderon, or Frida to
her friends, was an artist. She lived in sunny Mexico. Unlike
most artists whose work you might see in a gallery, Frida didn't
go to art school. Instead she taught herself. At this time, it
was thought that only men could become "serious artists."
Frida thought that was silly, so she didn't let it worry her.

While alone at home, she dreamed of fantastical scenes and turned them into magical paintings.

Frida liked to paint lots of outfits or versions of herself in the same picture. She did this to show what it was like to feel like lots of different people, all rolled into one body.

Sometimes she felt like she was a little child, and sometimes she felt like a grown-up.

When Frida was a child, she had an illness called polio, and then she had a terrible bus accident. This meant lots of time recovering in bed, which was very boring.

To cheer her up, her father made her a special easel. It meant she could paint while lying down. Frida had lots of illnesses in her life, and so she became used to painting this way.

Sometimes Frida felt on top of the world! When she felt like this, her paintings would be filled with sunny colors and Mexican plants from her garden.

Sometimes Frida felt low and frustrated that one of her legs was always more tired than the other. When she felt like this, her pictures were filled with gloomy colors.

Sometimes she felt happy and sad at the same time. When she felt like this, her paintings were filled with all sorts of colors!

At this time, the most famous artists in Mexico were mural painters who painted straight onto walls. The most famous of them all was Diego Rivera.

One day, Diego was painting near where Frida lived. She took one of her paintings to show him. As soon as he saw it, he could tell that Frida was a brilliant artist.

The pair became very close and inspired each other. In his work, Diego tried to show a world where everyone was equal. Frida wanted to put the same message into her paintings, too.

When they weren't painting, they campaigned for people of all races and abilities to be respected equally, and for poor people to be paid fairly.

Even though Diego was older than Frida and she called him her "ugly frog-toad," they fell in love. In the middle of summer, Frida and Diego were married in the town hall in Coyoacán, Mexico.

At this time, young married women in Mexico were expected to become mothers and full-time housewives. Frida already knew that she couldn't have children and she didn't let married life get in the way of her first love, which was painting.

Frida was fond of Mexican tradition, but
at times it could feel as stuffy as a
stiff, frilly dress, and not very "her" at all.

Although her paintings had parts that were realistic, people often said they looked like they were scenes from dreams or nightmares.

This annoyed Frida, who would say,
"I never paint dreams,
I paint my own reality."

Often her work is called "symbolism" because it is filled with symbols, or objects that have meanings. Sometimes her work is called "magic realism," because it shows objects from real life but with a big sprinkle of Frida's special magic!

Frida went to the USA with Diego because he had been asked to paint a new artwork. Frida loved meeting other glamorous artists who admired and encouraged her art, but she dearly missed Mexico.

Three years later, and still in the USA, Diego was enjoying success in New York and was painting lots of big murals.

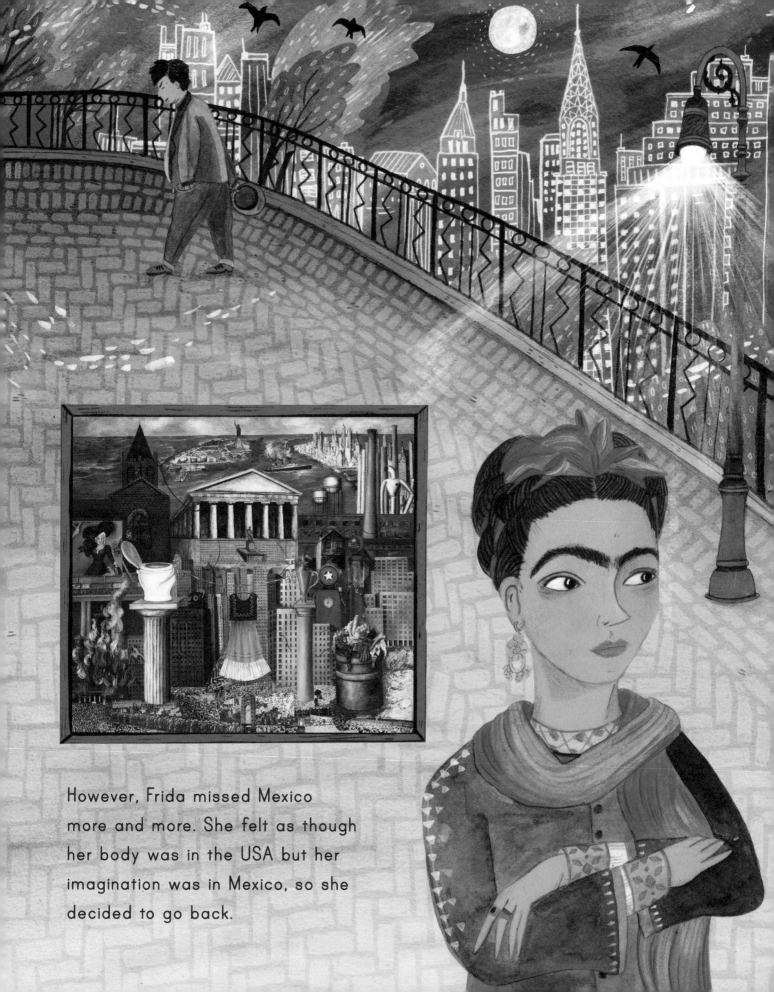

However, Frida missed Mexico
more and more. She felt as though
her body was in the USA but her
imagination was in Mexico, so she
decided to go back.

Frida was so happy to be back in Mexico that she painted more than ever before.

She was starting to become well known, and she managed to do something that no one from her country had ever done before—she was given her very own exhibition in New York City.

In Mexico, Frida made friends with a French poet named André Breton. He loved Frida's unusual painting of a bath and asked her to show her work to people in Paris. This was the first time her art had been so far away from Mexico.

The Louvre Museum in Paris bought a painting by Frida. She became the first Mexican artist in their gallery.

When Frida came back from Paris, Diego also came back to Mexico and the pair lived in the blue house, surrounded by lots of unusual animals. Many of Frida's animals can be spotted in her paintings.

When Frida died, she was still a young woman, but in her short life, she overcame many obstacles. She taught herself how to paint, and she became a famous woman artist in what seemed like a man's world.

MUSEO FRIDA KAHLO

Although her paintings touch people all over the world, Frida's heart will always be rooted in her beloved Mexico. You can still visit her bright blue house and see where she painted her masterpieces.

WHAT'S IN THE MASTERPIECE?

TREE OF HOPE, KEEP FIRM, 1946

Frida painted this after she had some painful surgery on her back. She is in the picture twice, first as herself just after the operation and second as a reminder that she will be back to her strong colorful self again.

WHAT THE WATER GAVE ME, 1938

This picture sums up lots of things that were important to Frida. It shows her legs in the bath, the legs that she loved despite the fact they gave her such trouble! In the water, she sees her family and places in Mexico.

FRIDA AND DIEGO RIVERA, 1931

When Frida painted this, she had been married to Diego for two years. She has deliberately painted herself looking very stiff. This is how people often looked in Mexican folk art, and Frida wanted to show how much it had inspired her.

SELF-PORTRAIT IN A VELVET DRESS, 1926

This is the first painting Frida made of herself. It is called a "self-portrait." Self-portraits are what Frida became most famous for, and she painted lots of them.

THE TWO FRIDAS, 1939

These women look like identical twins, but they are both Frida! She sometimes felt like two people at once. One Frida wears traditional clothes and the other wears bright colors. Their hearts are connected by one long vein.

THE WOUNDED DEER, 1946

This might remind you of a bad dream. The strange combination of real things in this kind of picture is called "surrealism" or "magic realism."

SELF-PORTRAIT ON THE BORDER BETWEEN MEXICO AND THE USA, 1932

In this picture, Frida stands on the line that divides Mexico (left) and the USA (right). Behind her are symbols that sum up what each country means to her. She holds tight to a Mexican flag showing where she truly feels at home.

MY PARENTS, GRANDPARENTS, AND I, 1936

Little Frida holds on to a red ribbon connecting her to her family tree. She stands in the middle of her blue house, the center of her world.

SELF-PORTRAIT WITH THORN NECKLACE AND HUMMINGBIRD, 1940

This scene shows Frida looking calm while thorny twigs cut her neck. It shows how she had grown used to pain after many years of illness. The hummingbird is an ancient Mexican symbol of love, and the panther is a symbol of bad luck.

ROOTS, 1943

Frida felt that Mexico gave her inspiration and life. In this picture, she grows from the Mexican soil and is nourished by her roots, just as a plant would be.

IMAGES CREDITS

Inspiring | Educating | Creating | Entertaining

Brimming with creative inspiration, how-to projects, and useful information to enrich your everyday life, Quarto Knows is a favorite destination for those pursuing their interests and passions. Visit our site and dig deeper with our books into your area of interest: Quarto Creates, Quarto Cooks, Quarto Homes, Quarto Lives, Quarto Drives, Quarto Explores, Quarto Gifts, or Quarto Kids.

First published in 2019 by Wide Eyed Editions, an imprint of The Quarto Group.
400 First Avenue North, Suite 400, Minneapolis, MN 55401, USA.
T (612) 344-8100 F (612) 344-8692 **www.QuartoKnows.com**

A catalog record for this book is available from the British Library.

ISBN 978-1-78603-642-1
The illustrations were created artwork created with traditional and digital media
Set in La Chic, Palomino Sans, and Print Bold

Published by Rachel Williams and Jenny Broom
Designed by Nicola Price
Edited by Lucy Brownridge
Production by Nicolas Zeifman
Picture research by Jen Veall

Manufactured in Guangdong, China TT052019

1 3 5 7 9 8 6 4 2